SAID THE RIVER

SAID THE RIVER

Poems by Liz Zetlin
Drawings by Janis Hoogstraten

Penumbra Press

Published by Penumbra Press with assistance from the Ontario Arts Council
and the Canada Council. The Publisher also thanks Stuart MacKinnon,
whose careful readings and attention assisted the author in rendering the
present text.

Printed in Canada by HBTechnoLith, Ottawa.

ISBN 0 921254 72 5   Paperback

Canadian Cataloguing in Publication Data

Zetlin, Liz, 1944-
    Said the River

(Penumbra Press poetry series : #41)
1st ed.
ISBN 0-921254-72-5

    1. Crawford, Isabella Valancy, 1850-1887 — Poetry.
I. Hoogstraten, Janis   II. Title   III. Series.

PS8599.E56S35 1995   C811'.54   C95-920964-6
PR9199.3.Z48S35 1995

Penumbra Press

Time is the substance from which I am made.
Time is a river which carries me along,
but I am the river, it is a tiger that devours me,
but I am the tiger, it is a fire that consumes me,
but I am the fire.

Jorge Luis Borges
Labyrinths

Isabella:
The River gazed at our strong, free ghosts
And with rocky fingers shed
Apart the silver curls of its head...

Susan:
How can you stand her florid verses?

Margaret:
Just look at her eyes.

Susan:
The saddest eyes I've ever seen, except maybe yours.

Margaret:
She's been haunting me since I saw her
name on the historical plaque in Paisley.
I don't know why I'm compelled to find her.
You've done white water, haven't you, Sue?

Susan:
Shouldn't be a problem, remember?
I took a three day course on the Magnetewan.

Margaret
Right, I forgot.

Contents

Part 1

Part 2

Part 3

Part 1

All dust in the wind of a woman's cry

Isabella Valancy Crawford
"The Rose of a Nation's Thanks"

Said the River—One

I am the fire that burns.
I am the tiger that consumes time.
I am all the time there is.

I begin as excess
as run off, eroding
my own bed, insistent
as tears engraving a face
abundant as arterial blood.
Trout leak out wordless
as thoughts, emptying me
from head to mouth.
I am always thinking.
I am not so often thought.

I am a run-on sentence never
stopping when you think I should
cracking and straining beneath you
as a lover does until you lose
your breath and become
(as much as you can)
a part of me, your minutes
running into your hours
as our sun goes down.

Step into me and you'll walk
in clouds and stars. They say
you cannot step twice
into the same one of me
just as you can never step
twice into yourself.

I trickle, boil
babble, cascade.
I swirl into eddies,
meander and overflow.
I propose and abandon.
I never apologize.
I convey, I bathe and I soothe.
I am the one who gives
and the one who takes away.

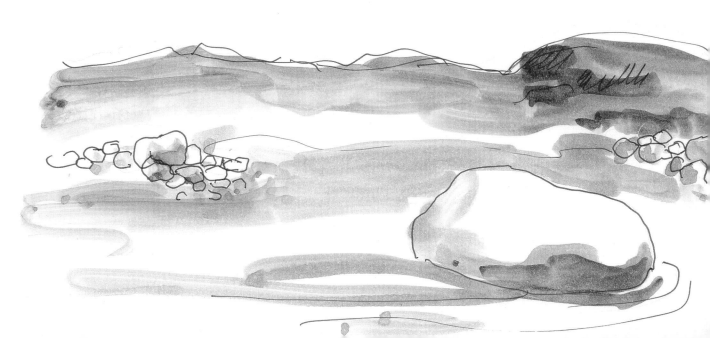

Apologies 1

They say Isabella died
in her landlady's arms.
In February. In Toronto.
Just six years after Pat Garrett
shot Billy the Kid. Even Jesse James
managed to live longer than she did.

She did not rob banks,
nor had she held up any trains,
though her father was accused
of embezzling from the town treasury.
Instead, she wrote long poems
about sorrow —*that dark matrix*,
about love in and of the wilderness,
about the *enslaved human tides*
on whose necks chaos would ride.

A weak heart, they said.
A February thaw followed
by a fierce storm.
A cold that wasn't bad enough
to keep her from leaving her room
at the corner of King and John
to deliver a poem to the *Globe*.

Had Isabella lived today, she might
have stayed inside on snowy days
e-mailing her poems around the world,
waiting for a child to die,
for the doctors to cut them open
and replace her own heart
with that of the child's.

They say her last words were

I'm sorry to be such a bother, Miss Stuart.

Sorry to be. Such a bother.
Isabella's apology still lingers,
waiting for someone to say

it's all right.

Collaborations

Any excuse for a canoe trip, thought Susan. A chance to draw and fish. And watch Margaret glue herself to another life.

Floundering around, Susan called it, as Margaret went from one obsession to another—from Emily Dickinson to Sylvia Plath and now back to the Victorian era again. Margaret has always headed backwards into another woman's life to look for her own. Her rooms wallpapered with her mother, her grandmothers, her great aunts. Her hair, too, takes on the style of her obsessions, from short and straight to long and permed and back to short again.

Now Margaret wanted help to search for a poet Susan had never heard of, to add her images to words Margaret would write. Well, maybe she could spare a few days in June.

Margaret had been to all of Susan LaFlame's shows—the big stain paintings, the landscapes, the plywood canoes, the fish series. She admired Susan's steady progress, her consistently short red hair, and even the white outline of a fish Susan had shaved behind her left ear. It all started in February. With jerk chicken and Bob Marley. To put us in the mood, they had said,

for moving over water

for imagining a book.

They talked of possible images, leafing
through a book luscious
with Chinese wood blocks.
How when they first looked,
each print on the left exactly
the same as the one on the right.
Mirror images of domestic chores.
Page after page.

Their eyes moved back and forth
from a Chinese woman with scarlet peonies
to scarlet peonies with a Chinese woman.
From fish to flower
flower to fish.

By the time they'd ordered a second Red Stripe,
they had discovered small variations.
A blue carp on the left page
became green on the right.
A woman's frown turned into a smile.
How they each looked at the same thing
yet remembered something different.
Yellow irises. Bound feet.
A dark line of shoulder.
How the mind selects small details—
        what to recall
        what to leave out.

Mothers

Sydney Crawford, mother of Isabella

February, 1876, Toronto

Isabella was my sixth child, yes
she made up the first half
of a baker's dozen—slid out eager
for her first taste of milk.
The only one without pain.
The afterbirth a silvery gray,
stitched with veins purple
as those on the back of my hand.

Her brother early too—
Stephen's head so small
it would have fit in a teacup.
I kept him in a wooden butter box
lined with cotton batting, beside the stove.
Isabella always slept next to me.
The only one I have left.
The only one I can count on.

Mine is a face for others to ignore.
No descriptions. No photographs.
I exist only through my daughter's eyes
in spite of all the graves
dug for my children
and by the grace of the linen
I embroider each night.

Darker the shadows that on me are sweeping,
Blood of my heart!

I.V.C.
"Mavourneen"

Sophie Anshen, Margaret's mother

November 7, 1987, North Carolina

Dear Margaret,
Long life and late births run in the family.
I was forty two when you were born.
My mother Sarah was born when Mary,
her mother, was fifty seven.
Did I ever tell you—Mary died
at the age of one hundred and four,
struck by lightening while feeding the chickens.
Love, mom

November 14, 1987

Dear one,
Just time for a note.
I seem to be between a dead calm
and a seething rage.
Writing this among a bouquet
of satisfactions and angers.
Is there a plant called anger?
If there isn't, there should be.
It would be an herb that grows wild
along the road and can only be propagated
by tornadoes, fire or flood.

my despairs—
       chest aches
       hard to breathe
       this reconciling

my satisfactions—
       a morning of pulling vines
       hunger reappears
       pruning the red maple
       marvelous for rage.

The mother's soul

Margaret remembers
watching her mother
undress inside
her walk-in closet

how her breasts had withered
lying there on her chest like blind
kittens waiting to be picked up
by the scruff of the neck

how her smell had become stronger
a musk lingering in her closet
saturating the house

how she must see herself
shrinking (though slower than her husband)
as she doesn't have as far to go

how her flax blue eyes still bloom
with dreams for her daughter
and for herself.

A mother's death

When the moon was horned the mother died,
And the child pulled at her hand and knee,
And he rubbed her cheek and loudly cried:
"O mother, arise, give bread to me!"
But the pine tree bent its head,
And the wind at the door-post said:
"O child, thy mother is dead!"

I.V.C.
"The Mother's Soul"

February 14, 1988

Dearest Margaret,
I've got a special file I want you to know about.
It's under "s" for Socrates.
The instructions are in the file.
If I ever get to where there is nothing
left, there are fifty pills under the mattress
to be taken with water. Then I start drinking
preferably martinis, but scotch would be easier.
You must burn this letter.
I'm counting on you.
Love, mom.

❦

As though it were as easy as making a cake—
        cream butter and eggs
        add flour and milk
        mix until smooth
        bake til a knife comes out clean.

Only her mother's recipe is even simpler—
        pills, water, scotch

A few steps her mother doesn't mention—
        hold her hand
        decide if you can do this
        (if you have the right)
        destroy the pill bottle
        call the doctor
        learn how to grieve
        how to know it's all right.

Treasures of a destroyed community

March 6, 1988

Dearest Margaret,
"There is a time to live and a time to die."
(The Bible is one of the few books
I can still bear to read.)
Please scatter my ashes on the water.
Thought you might like to see this catalogue
of ritual objects I got in New York.
xxxx, mom.

                              urns
                             scrolls
                    a silver circumcision knife
          an inscribed Torah bound in painted linen
                *I am sending an angel before you
                    to guard you on the way*

                 Long ago her mother had told her
                   she had met the survivors

                      a woman who had to
                      make lamp shades
                      out of human skin
                     and survived to laugh
                     and the guilty ones
                        who still dwell
                    on what they had to do
                       to stay alive.

Her mother's thumb

In one of Sophie's letters
Margaret read why she had been
sent away on Saturday mornings.
Her mother didn't want her to become
obsessed with faith.

By seeing ritual movements up close
Sophie supposed there would be
no mystery in the swaying of the robe,
the unrolling of the parchment scroll,
the repeated prayers, the lighting
of candles.

All those years Sophie was driving her daughter
to school, to the shoe store
to have spiked heels dyed to match a dress,
she had her own ritual movements.

Barely able to see above the steering wheel
Sophie gripped it with both hands,
her right thumb soon working itself
free. The thumb jerked up and down
as she drove, as they talked about shades
of pink, as they sat silent.

Margaret prayed her friends
wouldn't notice.
This was the only sign
her mother gave her then
a secret message even the sender
couldn't decode.

Margaret was witnessing
the inside of her mother
coming out, dancing
to an erratic rhythm, almost
as thought it didn't belong to her,
demanding its rightful place
even if only at the very
end of her.

She wanted to grab her mother's thumb,
stop it from jerking, force its energy
up her arm, across her shoulder
into her throat, where it would leap
into her voice.

How Margaret needed that voice
to tell her what possessed her so
and what there was (or could be)
to put her faith in.

No pain

Margaret was reading "The Mother's Soul"
when she got the call.

A stroke, the doctor said.
She flew to North Carolina.

A nurse was trying to feed her mother spoonfuls
of applesauce, catching the overflow and pushing
it back in. When Sophie saw her daughter,
one side of her mouth smiled.

"No pain," her mother said. "A kind of euphoria."
Only it sounded like "kin and fleurs."

She signaled for Margaret to sit beside her
and pushed the tray away.

Margaret sat in the darkened room.
The sun filtered through the blinds.

She remembered the letter.
Could she be depended on? She wasn't sure.
Her mother was counting on her.
And she wasn't sure.

But then it happened so fast, she was telling Susan,
at one of their lunches. Afterwards, by the side of her mother's bed, a note—

Classic Hebrew has only a present tense
the past and future
are indicated by a conjunction.

a convergence

a confluence

a covenant

Fathers

Dr. Stephen Dennis Crawford, Isabella's father

1862, Paisley

A dental turn-key in his right hand,
Dr. Crawford commands Simon Orchard
to open his mouth and quit complaining.
　　　　"You've brought the potatoes?"
　　　　Orchard nods.
　　　　Crawford tightens the handle and gives a quick tug.
　　　　Orchard squirms and moans.
　　　　"I'll pull every tooth in your head for the same price, just say the word."
　　　　Orchard shakes his head.
　　　　"What took you so long?" Dr. Crawford says to Isabella as she runs into the
room, her fingers stained from the raspberries she ate on the way through town. He
talks to his daughter and the mouth open beneath him, both the same height.
　　　　"They want me to pull their rotten teeth and slimy babies from their wives.
All I get for this woman's work," he says, turning to his daughter, "is a sack of
potatoes."
　　　　"Take them home to your mother, Isabella." and when she protests, saying
they're too heavy—"Hurry up, your mother's counting on you."

Dr. Milton Anshen, Margaret's father

1962, North Carolina

Dr. Anshen never speaks
of the lives he must have saved
or the deaths he must have seen.
But Margaret finds them abandoned
in the weave of his wool jacket,
crouched in his black leather bag
packed with needles and penicillin.
She sees them lying on her mother's good
china plates, next to the carrots and peas—
just another vegetable she has to finish
before she can be excused.
She wants to hear about these lives,
comfort him when the deaths come.

She listens to his voice deepen with sorrow
when she doesn't answer his questions
about what she's done at school that day—
her silence a punishment for his
unexplained anger, his silences
his unspoken love.
I'll tell you what *I* did all day,
he would say, his voice rising,
I looked up assholes.

His stout frame had already started to bend
when she was half his size,
first from raising her high
on his shoulders and later
for reasons she didn't understand.
Still proud and silent near the end,
he would not let her see him
struggling to figure out
how to plug in the reading light.

Sorting shapes

Dr. Crawford tells Isabella
he caught a colourless fish
one evening when the moon
was clouded over.

A slender shape
the length and width
of a hunting blade.
It was ugly he said,
I threw it back.

Isabella feels sorry
for this pale creature safe
only in the dark of the moon,
and thankful he has let it go.
Isabella looks down
to see her father crouched
by the foot of her bed
a pale shape the size of a trout
cupped in one hand.

She hears her father's voice
as though crooning a ballad—
you were born naked
as the white trout, you must hide
your love, my love
or they will destroy you
as they did me.

Sorting shoes

Margaret is touching her father's shoes.
She's never seen them without him inside.
Empty boats stranded at low tide.
His shirts hang freshly pressed
in a neat row above the shoes.
The older he got, the brighter
his clothes became.
He shrank inside them until
he was shorter than his daughter
and weighed even less.

"Pay cash and buy the best you can afford,"
he always told her.

She sees him beside his brand new
slate grey Buick, his car
and his shoes glowing like coals.
"If I had it to do over again," he is saying
"I would never have had children."
She has carefully framed this remark
next to his apple green shirts
and spit-shined shoes.

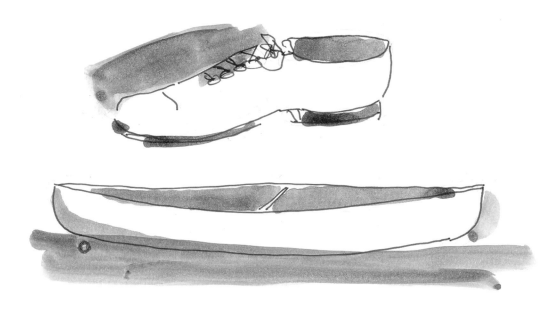

Part 2

Who curseth Sorrow knows her not at all.
Dark Matrix she, from which the human soul
has its last birth. . . .

I.V.C.
"Malcolm's Katie"

Hearts

Important. Record all activities and symptons in the Patient Activity Chart.
Do not tamper with the monitor in any way. Do not pull on the electrode leads
or disturb the tape holding the electrodes to your skin.

Halton Heart Monitor Instructions

Toronto General Hospital,
February, 1987

It's on the left side" Margaret says to the doctor.
"A swarm of bees buzzing in my chest.
I don't know, maybe five or six times a day."

For twenty four hours a cassette recorder
hangs from a surgical tube tied to the waistband
of Margaret's pants.

The tape records her heartbeats.
She records her activities and symptoms.

Activity	*Symptom*
sitting at reference desk	bored
answering phone	rushed
eating sandwich	dreaming of rivers
drinking coffee	fast heartbeat
walking home	tired
watching TV	irritated
trying to get to sleep	anxious
still trying to sleep	exhausted

Valentines Day, 1887

"The death of Isabella Valancy Crawford, which took place at 11:30 on Saturday night, was the result of heart disease and was quite unlooked for. Miss Crawford had been suffering from a cold for a fortnight past, but had not been confined to bed. She was retiring for the night, her mother being in the room, when she suddenly fell to the floor lifeless.

About ten years ago a medical man gave it as his opinion that the action of the diseased lady's heart was defective and as the complaint was hereditary, her father and a sister having died from the same cause, Miss Crawford was always careful to avoid over-exertion. When the fatal attack came on, a doctor was at once summoned, but on his arrival he pronounced life to be extinct."

The *Globe,* February 14, 1887

Apologies 2

I am of mingled Scotch, French and English descent, born in Dublin, Ireland. I was brought to Canada by my parents in my earliest childhood, was educated at home, and have never left my home but for about a month, that amount of absence being scattered over all my life. I have written largely for the American Press, but only published one volume on my own account "Old Spookses Pass, Malcolm's Katie and Other Poems" which appeared in 1884 in Toronto and is decorated with press errors as a Zulu chief is laden with beads. Voila tout.

Autobiographical sketch
Isabella sent the year before she died
to "Seranus," an editor of *The Week*

Apologies 3

Frequently sick
with headaches and chills
we drank vinegar
and laced our gowns
even tighter

      frail
    fainting
 easily diseased

science later taking over
the naming of our ills

an orex ic
ag or a pho bic

Imprisoned in our fathers'
houses, poems hidden
in kitchen cabinets,
our thoughts petrified
like flies in amber.

    delicate
     intact
  inaccessible

  through layers
   of absence.

Layers of absence

Margaret is tired of being caught
between the people who ask the questions
and the many sources of answer—
       what to reveal
       what to leave out.

After each question, she makes a pencil mark
on a scrap of paper, until it is covered
with tiny sticks that turn into sections
of picket fence.

Where are the books on gardening?
slash

When was Diefenbaker born?
 slash.

Why don't you have any new mysteries?
slash

Where is the washroom?
a mark across.

No one ever asks "Where is Isabella?"

She marks four sections of picket fence—
the number of years she has worked at the library.
Two more sections and she can retire.

For a long time now, she has been
afraid to look too closely.
For when she does, things grow
out of all proportion,
they overwhelm her.
She looses track, she's accused
of being vague, and then what
is she supposed to do?
Rivers' names repeat themselves
       Saugeen
       Teeswater
       the Don
She returns to them over and over,

trying to place herself there.
Thinking you can drown in rivers,
though that is almost too easy.
Better to float through other people's lives,
answer their questions instead of your own.

Other times it's words—
        vagabond
        ragamuffin
        mudlark
She travels on them like rivers.
Afraid she will have to change somehow,
in a way that is unknown to her now,
to complete this search for Isabella.

Change: crooked
          bent—with basic idea to turn

She could bend her life
but could she turn it around.

"Can't you speed it up any?"
a smooth-faced boy asks, chewing
on the ends of his hair.

Archives

Boolean searches
bibliographies,
newspapers, periodicals,
unpublished PHD theses.
All you have to do is follow the clues
back to the original source.
                    —Margaret's notes

Clue #1—passion

Mrs. Hefferman—formerly Miss Stuart, the Crawford's landlady—wrote:

"I was a young girl at the time of her death, but how could I forget one like Miss Crawford! She seemed to me like a being from another planet....She and her mother lived almost completely by themselves during the years that they lodged with us, except for one or two friends. But they had their own pursuits. They were deeply interested in English and European literature and would speak French together constantly. I used to watch her make her wonderful Irish potato pancakes on our kitchen table while she described the whole process to me in the language I was trying hard to learn. I think she was really gay at heart, but at times seemed sad and depressed. Her passion for music was almost as great as her love of books and poetry..."

Clue #2—headaches

Margaret signs in with the security guard and gains access to the past. The room is jammed with card catalogues and wooden tables for researchers. She starts with Crawford, which produces no entries, then finds a reference to Paisley.

A man in a white coat brings her an album. Here she feels the weight of history, laboratory of the past. Hoping for intimate revelations, she finds only comings and goings.

After trying desperately to read an unidentified "Diary of a trip from Collingwood to Fort William via Lake Superior on the steamer Algoma" because it was written in 1867, Margaret's head aches. The handwriting is so difficult to read, a jigsaw puzzle with pieces missing.

Clue #3—houses and grave stones

Upstairs in the photo archives, there is a light table for viewing negatives.
Margaret checks the subject headings—

Indians, ships, dentistry, pioneer life, medicine, mills, women

She makes her request. The librarian returns with three small grey cardboard
boxes with hinged lids and black metal brackets reinforcing the corners.

Put these on, he orders, handing Margaret a pair of white cotton gloves.

She views the Crawford country estate in Dublin and a six foot celtic cross of
grey granite marking Isabella's grave in the Little Lake Cemetary in
Peterborough with the inscription

Isabella Valancy Crawford
Poet
by the gift of God

The Baldwin Room

Margaret takes the subway to Yonge and Bloor. She walks north past Britnell's Books into the Metro Toronto Reference Library, past the fabric waterfall and up four flights of stairs to the Baldwin Room, a special collection of Canadiana. More houses and graves, she suspects.

The card catalogues reveal nothing about Isabella, just something called a scribbling book. Written in 1885 by a Winchester, Ontario woman named Emma. A delicate pencil script flows over the faded pages sewn with thin twine and knotted in the middle. Margaret begins to read the diary:

Must try and work at lace today....

The room turns grey, then ochre—the lights blink off and on. Two hours have passed, Margaret suddenly realizes, feeling as though she's mired in another memory lapse. Her notebook is now full of penciled notations.

Downstairs by the fabric waterfall she re-enters the late 20th century, opens her purse for the security guard, then walks over to the Morissey Tavern, where she orders a beer and begins to read her notebook.

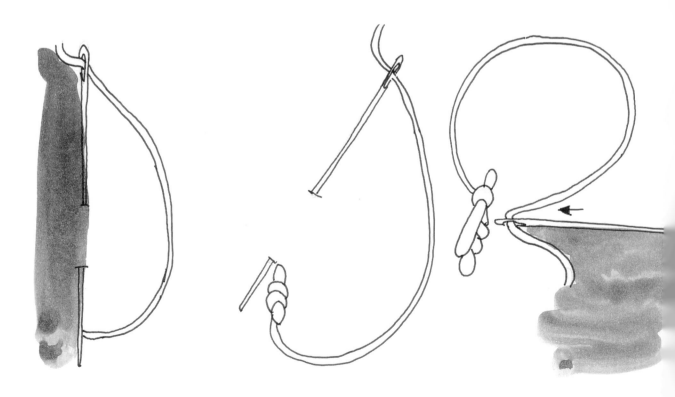

A mother's cry

She died as easily as she was born. Mrs. S was bringing her a pot of tea. All I heard was Mrs. S screaming. By the time I got there, Mrs. S was on the floor, holding Isabella's head in her lap. I wasn't even able to hold her in my arms before she was gone. My last child. How will I manage without her?

"You have sent me an angel, dear God," I used to say when she played the piano. But she would not practise when I told her.

I want to listen to the way words sound, she would say.

Her music was the scratching of pen and the flow of cold black ink. I told her she was being wasteful, writing instead of becoming a proper lady.

She said words slid out of her as easily as children out of me. Once the cord is knotted and cut, she said, children and stories are on their own. So many die of the fever or from neglect.

But the worst was yet to come. It wasn't the newspapers that were unkind. I committed to memory what The Evening Telegram said: *Miss Crawford was a young lady of marked ability and native wit*. An admirer even sent a wreath of white roses with the title of one of her poems "The Rose of a Nation's Thanks" embroidered on the ribbon. Now there's a man she might have married.

After I lost her, I took to my bed. Mrs. S visited me twice a day, bringing tea and scones. Last night, we found them. Mrs S slipped on the bare floor and fell onto Isabella's bed, spilling the tea. I hadn't yet removed the sheets, the old blue ones we brought with us from Peterborough. Stripping them off, Mrs. S must have felt something underneath, because she lifted up the corner of the mattress.

"Look, Mrs. Crawford," she exclaimed. Mrs. S reached under the mattress and handed me a thin notebook with the words "Scribbling Book" in large letters on the cover.

Beside the notation *this belongs to...* was her dear name, written in a firm script which still brings tears to my eyes—Isabella Valancy Crawford.

"There must be at least a baker's dozen of these," Mrs. S. said, reaching further back.

"Bring them here, Mrs. S. These are my daughter's finest works, of that I'm sure."

Burnt poems

Mrs. Crawford opened the scribbling book. The words smudged when she moved her fingers across the page.

Must try and work at lace today. I have so much to do this afternoon and am half sick with cold, my poor nose is fairly raw.

Thank you Mrs. Stuart. I'll be fine now. Just bring me the rest of the notebooks. Reading them will help me get to sleep. And please light the lamp.

Saturday, June 25, 1875
Pleasant weather though hot. Too warm for quilting, have postponed that. Mother made jelly. Strawberry and rhubarb. Naomi was ill again today. Spitting blood. It breaks my heart to see her so faint.

July 7
Of loud, strong pines his tongue was made;
His lips, soft blossoms in the shade—

Must finish this later—the Ss are here.

So she did write poems in these notebooks. Prayerfully, there will be some new ones I can send to *The Globe*.

Tuesday, July 19
Mrs. K at it again. They say the operation should have helped, but she still tries to burn her clothes whenever they leave her alone.

Fire her only weapon. Mother used thread. I still remember, though I could only have been five or six. My scribbler in my lap, she thought I had fallen asleep waiting for father to come home. The door opened. I heard him say —
        Come here woman, give the doctor his medicine.

Mother stood up, hands on her hips, as he walked towards her.

        Get me a drink, wife, he said.
        All tenderness gone from his voice.

You've had enough already, Mother said, hands leaving her hips, moving up to her face too late to block his hand. She fell backwards against the table, knocking the bread pudding to the floor. He stumbled into the bedroom and stood at the foot of their bed. I could hear him sigh as he relieved himself all over the quilted bedding.

Mother's face shone bruised and ashamed, a rough moon.

I saw her choose her two best sheets from the cedar chest. From her sewing box she took the longest needle, threaded it with blue cotton. She went into the bedroom.

Like Penelope she was up all night. She used her best chain and loop stitches. Tiny french knots. I wondered if she too would undo her work.

When the sky lightened, father was completely bound with a tight stitched line that appeared and disappeared all around the edges.

Mother had fallen asleep in the children's room.

I found the wet sheets in a heap on the floor. I thought I saw the outline of a stitched trout leaping from one corner of the pale blue sheet.

Nothing but lies. I would never do such a thing.
This comes from reading too many novels.
She's giving me another of my headaches.

❦

Thursday, July 21
Last night, I spread my hair out over the pillow. Shut my eyes. Crossed my hands over my chest. I thought if you saw me, mother, you would think how good I was. You used to tell me I was your angel. You would wrap me up in your arms. Hold me for hours, rocking. One night a steady pressure woke me up. Your arms were around me, your mouth sucking and kissing my throat. I was so ashamed. You wanted a lover, mother, not an angel.

What nonsense! I had no need for love.
I had my children.

"Mrs. S come stoke the fire!"

September 14 1878
Mother is making soap today. Down by the lake I saw cows and sheep floating by. Poor Mrs. K is crazy again. Monday morning she was dancing and carrying on up the street. They had quite a time to get her home. Mother says they will have to take her insides out to stop her dancing.

Where did you hear such a thing? It was hysteria, that's what the doctor said.
No wonder they had to operate. Imagine dancing after burning down your own house.

December 26, 1878
I was twenty eight yesterday. I am becoming quite ashamed of my age, the only
consolation being that it is not anything to be really ashamed of, despite what mother
says. Why is it that old-maidenhood is considered little short of a crime. Well, it would
not do for me to change my condition. I truly believe that the cares and responsibilities
of married life would make me wretchedly unhappy.

I could have looked after the children. You could have written every day and not
had to worry if your stories came back or if your prize money was lost.

August 1, 1879
Visited the Mechanics Institute again. The Globe hasnt printed my poem yet. I
happened to come across a leather bound volume by a Dr. Brodsky.

Recognizing the name, as mother had often talked of a Dr. Brodsky, I took the book from
the shelf. It was full of medical histories of women. There was a Mrs. C. who suffered
from violent headaches. Could that be mother?

Mother used to take to her bed for days, shutting the curtains. Dr. Brodsky suspected the
headaches started when Mrs. C's husband had a heavy bout of drinking. Dr. Brodsky
described her headaches —

> *the talented-but -thwarted headache*

> *the beautiful-but-neglected-by-her-husband headache*

> *the charming-to-friends but not-to-family headache.*

One night, Mrs. C. stole out of the house and walked for miles through the snow in her
nightdress. Screeching white witches flew in her path, their voices growing louder and
louder. She ran quietly over the snow, hands covering her ears, through the forest and
down by the river. In the morning she was found asleep on her doorstep.

The doctor's account stops here.

Yesterday before dawn, I walked down to the lake shore to watch the sun colour the
lake. When I returned, I found mother in a heap on the door step. I shook her. She
woke with a start and stumbled into the house. "They're after me" she said, to the chairs
and sofa. "Why are they screaming?"

"Why are you looking at me like that Mother?" I pleaded.
But she just turned away.

Mrs. Crawford threw the notebook on the bare pine floor, and closed her eyes, the headache settling in.

The Morrisey

When Margaret looked up from her notebook, Susan was walking past the bar. Beers ordered, Margaret read her notes to Susan. The menu planning for their canoe trip could wait.

"Where in the hell do these stories come from?" Susan asked, intrigued by her friend's bizarre stories.

"I found them in the library," Margaret said, not looking Susan in the eye. "Burnt poems, I call them."

"Burnt?"

"Someone must have destroyed Isabella's journals—I figure it was her mother. Probably threw them in the woodstove. Grandchildren is what she would have wanted, not the truth."

Margaret wouldn't admit she didn't know where these stories had come from.

Had she dreamed them?
Had they come from Emma's scribbling book?
Or could these be her own stories? Or her mother's?
Or was it Isabella guiding her hand?

Years ago Margaret's mother Sophie had told her
"I found my mother in a book."

"Is that where mother's are to be found?"
Margaret says to herself.

"What?" Susan asks.

Nothing.

"Talking to yourself again?" Susan taunts, her laughter echoing in the empty bar. "Come on, she says, when she sees the look on Margaret's face, "I'll buy you another beer."

Corner of King and John

Margaret has been meaning to take the streetcar to work . This way she can ride past the house Isabella died in, at the corner of King and John. She isn't sure if the new construction around the Dome Stadium has left the house still standing.

While waiting for the King car, she notices a woman on the sidewalk, looking west, her lean face almost harsh.

"Where is it?" Margaret hears her say. "Tell me, my good woman, where is John Street?"

"First of all, you're looking the wrong way," Margaret says, not so sure she likes the demanding tone of this stranger.

And besides, she looks odd. Tight laced boots like the punks wear, a long sleeved blouse with ruffles around the neck, hair piled on top of her head. The hottest summer in a hundred years, and this woman is dressed from head to toe in some kind of heavy fabric—cotton or linen maybe.

"Answer me! I've got to get back home," she insists.

"Take it easy, here comes the streetcar. Just get on when I do."

The woman lifts up her skirt and steps aboard, giving a coin to the driver.

"In the box, lady! Two bucks or you're off at the next stop."

Margaret drops in an extra token and follows the woman down the aisle.

"Thank you," the woman says to Margaret.
"I guess I've been away too long."

Where have you been? Margaret almost asks, turning towards the woman, whose sigh, she decides, is too deep to question.

Margaret sits in an aisle seat, reaches into her library book bag and pulls out Isabella's *Collected Poems*. She is rereading them to find quotes she can use in the book.

She underlines *I have made your heart my garden* and dog-ears the page with a twinge of guilt.

"My poems!" the woman cries, in astonishment. And then says in a hushed tone, which Margaret later realizes must have been gratitude, "You're reading my poems."

Margaret turns and rises quickly from her seat. Isabella's book slides from her lap into the aisle. She takes a deep breath and stares at Isabella.
"Yes," she says, "your poems."

The streetcar is passing through the canyons of the financial district. Workers have already swept up the birds that crashed into the glass and marble towers during the night. Peregrine falcons look for ledges to build their nests.

The roses of her young feet turn to flame,
Isabella chants to herself.

"Whose feet?" Margaret asks, and then holds her breath.

Close domes of marble rich with gold...
Isabella chants, louder.

Oh, you mean the banks? They're the only things made of marble or gold these days.

There's one—white Italian marble, Margaret adds, pointing to First Canadian Place, over sixty stories high. In its shadow, men and women carrying briefcases rush to work, stepping around the bodies lying on sidewalks wide as the underground river beds.

Famine cringes past. Isabella fortells.
So little space!—we starve—we faint—we die!

Margaret grabs Isabella's hand. "Come on, we've missed our stop."

Margaret drags Isabella to the middle of the car, down the steps onto the street, at the intersection of Bay and King. She leads Isabella back towards the direction they came from—where Isabella's rooming house should be.

She moves to meet the centuries. As they walk along, Isabella keeps reciting lines from her poems about Toronto. *The pulses of dead merchants stir in her. All dust in the wind of a woman's cry.* She doesn't seem to hear Margaret.

As though everyone else were struck dumb and she is the only one with the power of speech. Surrounded by white and gold towers shining like rivers.

Here it is, number 57, Margaret says, and tugs Isabella's sleeve to get her attention.

My scribbling books, Isabella says as she enters the restaurant on the first floor, *I must find my scribbling books.*

Margaret rushes up to the cashier, who is ringing in two breakfast specials. "The key, please, we need the key to the third floor." And adds, pointing to Isabella, who stands chanting in front of the homemade pies, "She used to live here."

I don't care if she's the Queen of England, she can't get upstairs. No one can." He leans across the counter and whispers to Margaret, "They say it's haunted."

"But we've come from so far away," she pleads. "See how tired my friend is." She turns to point to the spot where Isabella was standing, but no one is there.

Just a dirty glass case full of apple, cherry and coconut cream pies.

Margaret runs out yelling Isabella's names—all three of them—but there is no response.

She walks south past the headquarters for the Canadian Broadcasting Company. At the end of John Street, she notices a new parkette beside the Dome Stadium. Stunned by Isabella's appearance, and a little out of breath, she sits down on a wooden bench to rest.

Death, Margaret reads in her mind.

The words appear etched. A coal black script carved into pink granite.

Then out loud she says *my death.* My death. There's something courageous about those two words together, she decides. The only thing that is truly ours. That belongs to us in a way words and children don't.

Navigator. This word appears in helvatica bold.

One that travels by water. Steers a course. Navigator of knowledge—that's what she's supposed to be.

Leaving the park, Margaret doesn't notice the shiny brass plaque that says

Isabella Valancy Crawford Park

Part 3

My masters twain the slaughtered deer
Hung on forked boughs with tongs of leather:
Bound were his stiff, slim feet together,
His eyes like dead stars cold and drear.

I.V.C.
"Said the Canoe"

Mirrors 1

Margaret keeps checking the rear view mirror
to make sure Susan is following close behind her.

She just has to glance up, the past is there
enclosed by the present.

That's how her mind works. In reverse.
Obsessed by reflections from the past.
These visions appear suddenly, as she turns the corner,
like the distorted view of her own body that looms
in the fish eye mirror
of her neighbourhood variety store.

The section of mind she looks through to see
what is out there, what awaits her—this part,
which should be at least the size of her windshield—
is not even as big as her car's rear view mirror.

She is losing something. Being eroded away.
Without knowing how or why, but suspecting
this force has the strength of water and the ability
to take many forms.

Mirrors 2

Glancing in the rear view mirror, Margaret sees a pink arm
emerge to tap on the side of Susan's green canoe.
A Bluewater Saugeen, the perfect craft
for their trip down a river of the same name.

Between car and canoe, this interruption of flesh
seems out of place. Margaret laughs out loud.
Imagines Susan might use this image
as the cover for their book.

The Saugeen—interrupted by flesh

The title, Susan had insisted,
was Margaret's responsibility.

Maybe it should have something to do with canoes.
Susan does big paintings of canoes.
Last summer she had gone out alone for two weeks
on Lady Evelyn Lake and from memory,
made a series of pastel drawings.
Stages of travel through the wilderness.
A record of Susan's vision of the land.
How a story changes
from the moment of experience
to the retelling of a memory.

What happens, Margaret wonders, now that she's gone
beyond living memories? What will she find?
Wouldn't that depend on how she goes about looking?

The best she could come up with was her words.
They had agreed the trip would dictate the rest.
And perhaps it was this vagueness
that made them eager
and at the same time anxious.

Already some forces at work.
Skimming the same road.
Only they are in two separate cars.
And there is a time lag.
Everything that Margaret sees,
Susan is seeing just after her—

a year-round trailer park
the bloody remains of some large animal

Margaret's stomach contracts and she wonders
if Susan will feel the same revulsion.

Even in childhood, their friendship
had seemed to need a certain distance,
a respect for small details
unexplained obsessions.

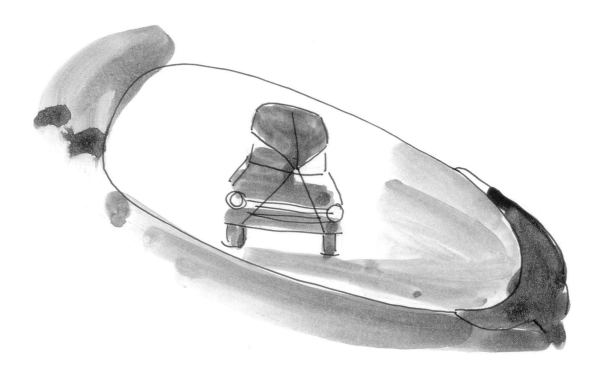

Evidence . . .

On the highway north of Toronto, Susan reaches out the window to test the straps holding down the canoe. A little loose, but they should hold. She sees her friend's frizzed hair above the seatback. Why is she obsessed by this woman, what's her name—Elizabeth? What does she expect to find? Always setting off on some project and abandoning it midstream. Will she finish this one?

If anything ever happened to Margaret, Susan muses, I would make a piece in her honour. Some place where it would be seen by lots of people. Like the aisle of a large supermarket. People will look at anything when they're shopping.

Maybe a life-sized cut out of a middle-aged woman holding eight rolls of non-bleached toilet paper. The title of our book would be printed on the woman's T-shirt and she would have a sign in one hand saying that both papers had been recycled. There would be one of these women in front of each check-out counter, next to the magazines.

Susan laughs and turns up the volume of her radio.

. . . of a past presence

There never flew across the violet hills
A morn so like a dove with jeweled eyes
                              I.V.C.
                              "Said the Daisy"

We're just about on top now. Must be one of the high points
of Ontario, Margaret thinks, as she shifts into third.
Yes, there's the sign. White letters
on a brilliant blue background

                  Violet Hill

Where the road curves to the right and I can barely
take my eyes off the lime and lemon hills.
In and out in sixty seconds.
Violet Hill, pseudonym for a town.
But it's the sky that looks violet, not the hills.
Has Susan ever been here before?
Does she know how special this place is to me?
Not just the name of the town,
but the power coming from the hills.

"Violet Hill," Susan says to herself as she sees the sign.
Great name for a town.
I can feel a kind of electrical charge
coming from the earth.
Looks like an orchard, except instead of trees,
there are little mounds growing all over the place.
As though someone had planted fields of women
lying on their backs with only their breasts sticking up.
All jumbled on top of each other.
Must have sprouted out of the ground,
but nobody knows they are there.
Just the violet hills a dead give-away.

As she drives, Susan outlines the violet hills
with alizarin on a brush dipped in Chinese white.
She recalls the topographical map
her father kept tacked up in the kitchen.
Wavy blue lines, too many to count,
and two large blue patches separating
the land from itself. The prairie land,
she had found out, was as flat as the map.

She had drawn heavy red lines around
the borders of her province, except
at the top right side, where it was sculpted
by Hudson Bay. This edge she left unmarked.
Sometimes that corner looked like the profile
of a large face crushed by the fierce passion of
a smaller face leaning down.

Using shades of green, she coloured areas of tundra,
grass and evergreen trees. Gentle strokes,
small precise movements of the wrist.
The pencil held lightly as the point rounded.
She filled up the whole country with saffron,
Prussian blue, pthalo green and copper red.

Historical plaque

Margaret walks behind the plaque,
onto the bridge and leans over the rail.
She looks down the Saugeen River
as it runs through the town of Paisley.

Stretching further over the edge, she stares
into the water. The reflection of the plaque
seems to blend with the river, the plaque
and the river both the same golden brown.
Bronze letters suspended in liquid.
Isabella's name rests on Margaret's own
ragged shadow.

As though the words have slid off
their metal backing and settled
onto the surface of the river. Floating
yet not moving downstream as a twig
or mayfly would.

Suspended. A tempting bait.

Arrive

The two women sit on the banks of the Saugeen. Looking for Isabella's presence, they will travel from Paisley to the river's mouth at Southampton.

>   three women
>   all in the river together
>   each at the same time
>   each in her own time
>
>   wary of the river
>   and perhaps each other
>   they joke

Got to make sure when we leave a car
at Southampton, that we come back to Paisley
in the right one.

Susan looks puzzled.
Oh, you mean the one with the canoe on top!

They laugh hysterically and for a long time.
Bring the one with the canoe on top!

>   small lapses
>   ineptitudes
>   vulnerabilities exposed

Susan is afraid of moths.
Bug dope leaks out all over
Margaret's pants.
Other secrets kept to themselves
        Margaret's encounter with Isabella
        Susan's fear of being abandoned

        a mythology develops

They have arrived—
inhabitants of the river bank
using the same stream as Isabella,
as many others before them,
sitting on land too often touched.

Derive

They sit in the fairgrounds drinking rum from tin cups,
staring across the river. On the opposite shore
are a few trees. The most obvious landmark a large trailer
parked high on top of the hill.

They talk of the river, how the only danger
they anticipate is the fast water, as they are mainly
lake travelers unaccustomed to swollen streams.
They don't talk about what Margaret waits for—
            some message, evidence of a past presence,
            or what Susan fears.

Their laughter blends with the sounds
of rum flowing over ice and tin
and the rising of the Saugeen.

                As the sun sets, as the sky darkens
and the stars come out, the trailer appears to shine
with a warm eerie glow. Reflected light
from the baseball field, they suppose.
They expect lights to come on in the trailer,
but none do.
                A dog barks. Fireflies blink
on and off in front of the white cedars.

When the field lights go off, the trailer dims.
Then one side of the trailer gets brighter.
            Then the other.
            They watch in silence.

"Did you notice," Margaret finally asks,
"how it brightens and dims?
            Even after the field lights went off?"

"From one side to the other." Susan says.
            "You saw it too?"

They are reassured.
As though each has seen the same vision.
At that moment, they could have believed anything.

Margaret wonders if Isabella might be sitting
inside the trailer, watching them. Margaret is afraid
she has somehow caused this diversion, the aluminum glow
a reflection of her vagueness. Afraid the trailer's presence
would be more powerful than Isabella's.

Fascinated by the trailer as icon, Susan borrows
a piece of paper from Margaret's notebook
and does a quick pencil sketch.

> a rectangle on top of a curling line
> > three triangles
> small dots for the fireflies and the stars

How could a house on wheels be more important?

Where is Isabella?

Derived

flowing from
drawing off water from
          taking
from a specified source
                    —Webster's

As they sit on the river bank
each woman pretends
to hold a book in her lap
turns imaginary pages
judges the right size and shape
to balance on knees and thinks
how the pages should
sound like rapids
how they should light up
like fireflies.

Ladies don't read

Isabella dangles her feet in the river and reads
from a book she found in the Paisley Town Hall:

How to be a Lady, A Book for Girls

I can think of nothing more injurious to the young
than spending their leisure hours in bending
over novels. Not only is the health injured by such means,
but the mind loses it vigour. If you once become
accustomed to such reading, you will find it produces
a kind of 'moral intoxication' so that you will feel
as uneasy without it as the drunkard without his cups,
or the smoker without his pipe."

Reading the Map

Carefully they unfold the large topographical map and the land
lies in front of them described and catalogued.
In the upper left-hand corner is a large patch of blue
labeled Lake Huron. The rest of the map is white,
with patches of green (wooden areas, orchards and vineyards),
grids of orange (red and black lines for the roads)
and a curving blue for the rivers.

The towns of Paisley and Southampton are pink.
Even in this printed form the earth's energy radiates.
They study the glossary of things likely to be found—
> abandoned
> monastery
> proposed
> ruins
> trout farm
> underground stream

Margaret wonders what an *abandoned* is.
Susan, a *proposed*.
"Will we find any?" they ask each other.

Using the space held open between thumb
and forefinger, Margaret measures the river's length.
Susan suggests a map wheel, more exact,
kind of like drawing, she says.

Hold it like a pencil, run it backwards
to return the dial to zero. It's important
to start a trip from the beginning.
Put it on the place you want to leave. Trace a path
along the river, its detours and oxbows,
all that snaking back on itself until
you reach the place you want to be.

If only finding that place were as simple as tracing a line.
Was that the reason? To trace a life, feel its contours
under their hands, starting from the end

> *sorry to be such a bother*

and hoping to find not just the beginning,
but all that middle.

Starvation year

Bruce County, 1858

After a severe drought, no rain fell from June 23 to August 11.
Many families lost everything.

On August 11 of starvation year, the records show Mrs. Sydney Crawford
bought two Crown lots in Paisley for fifty dollars from the Walkerton Land
Registry offices—lots 17 and 18 on Regent Street South.

There was no explanation as to why Mrs. Crawford was allowed to buy land.
Only men over eighteen could be landowners. Was this because her husband
was a doctor? Did she purchase it in his stead? Or perhaps she had come to
the registry office dressed as a man.

all we know for certain
is that it rained
all the next day
and as the rain
moistened the fields
and flooded the rivers
this may have been the day
when Isabella first held
the river
in her mouth

Opposite shores

Then came smooth-coated men with eager eyes.

I.V.C.
Malcolm's Katie

Simon Orchard must have been a man
used to shaping his destiny.
In the Bruce county histories
his hair sticks straight up
as though he had squeezed it
into clumps, forcing it to take shape
the way he did the rivers.

His thick wide lips
would never have mouthed
the words *I'm sorry.*

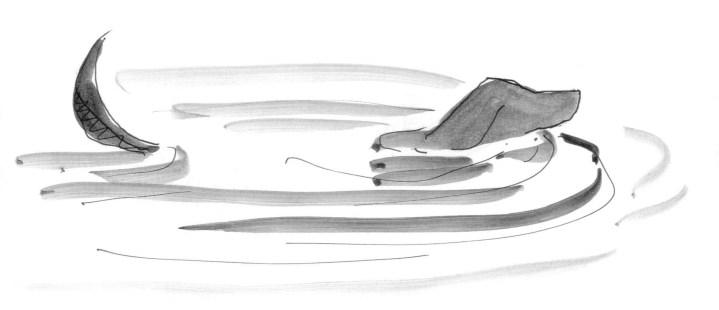

Even in his dreams, he knew what he wanted—
a place where two rivers come together.
His wild-eyed look must have come from nights
spent listening for the rush of waters.

Floating his family down the Saugeen,
Simon would have seen low rolling hills,
plum trees blooming a mass of white,
flocks of passenger pigeons blackening the sun.
In one unbroken column they flew
like some great river, like thunder,
like a storm, like a train, until softly
they landed on the fields and trees
only to be carried off by the wagon load,
their feathers stuffing potholes
their small bodies abandoned
or baked into pigeon pie.

It couldn't have taken Simon more than a day
to reach the spot where the Teeswater
joined the Saugeen. With his raft's cedar logs,
he built the first bridge and a village named
Paisley sprung up around him.

Simon trained Danger to swim
messages across the river.
Come here boy, here Danger, here Danger.
Tail wagging, Danger fights the current,
climbs the muddy bank and drops a bottle
at Samuel's Rowe's feet, the dog's shivering
covering Simon's brother-in-law with a fine spray.
Inside the bottle were simple messages:

More nails for the Crawford house.
A new axe blade.

"Do dogs remember?" Margaret asks?
"Yes," Susan says, "but they do not remember
that they remember."

27

Paisley — 1860's

Sabbath morn saw the Crawfords among
the church-going villagers, the doctor dignified
in his morning coat, gray plug hat and ivory-headed cane;
his wife in Irish poplin and Paisley shawl and bonnet
tied with brown ribbon, and the little Isabella in hoop skirt
of tartan plaid with dainty frilled pantalettes, beaver cloth coat
and blue satin hat; the trio followed at a respectable distance
by Maggie, the faithful nurse, with frail little Naomi by the hand.

Mrs. Annie Sutherland,
Samuel Rowe's, granddaughter,
whose pen name was "Antrim."

Paisley — 1990's

Isabella's absence encircles Margaret
like a deep-fringed shawl woven
from rivers she must have travelled
homes she would have entered
and sculptures she embroidered
with an elephant and three turbaned Hindus—
    one with a stick
    one with a feather
    and one steadying the sides
    of a blue tasseled howdah
and on top of the elephant a boy and a girl
back to back edged with a border of x's
that stand not for kisses but for the times
women embroidered their lives
with only a needle to push the sharp point of them
through the years

and for the times Margaret has been wrapped
by absence, that disturbing warmth
of shawl around shoulder

the kind of warmth
lacking any human touch.

Counting words

A tall dark young woman...one whom most people
would find difficult, almost repellent in manner.
But her work charmed me, though I had to tell her,
she declares, still regretful after all the years, that
we didn't pay for poetry.

—Seranus, describing
Isabella's visit to her office at "The Week"

Isabella learned addition by counting her brothers
and sisters. In front of her were five. Then came six
or seven more, the spaces between them becoming
smaller, like the shortening intervals
between lightning and thunder.

In one week typhus, or maybe it was black
diphtheria, made her take away seven.
Before she was even eight years old, she had
mastered subtraction. After her brother went
north, she subtracted her father from the count.

Just two left— one on either side of her.
Emma Naomi, her younger sister. Sydney Scott, her mother.
Three women. The magic number of fairy tales and myths.

Finally, after Naomi was gone, she counted
her own words. Short of paper, she wrote all the way
to the margins and between the already close lines.
As she added up her words, she placed the sum
at the end of each stanza. Her words like stitches,
marks made to please, to make pretty, to bind.

In winter, Isabella warmed the frozen ink bottle
with gloved hands, only removing her gloves
to eat potato pancakes at breakfast and dinner.

Margaret had nothing much left to count.
No brothers or sisters, her mother and father gone.
A man who had settled into passions other than her.

She was counting on Isabella for connections.
And on Susan as witness.

Or did she mean Susan to be the connection, Isabella the witness.

The Lily Bed

His cedar paddle, scented, red,
He thrust down through the lily bed;

Cloaked in a golden pause he lay,
Locked in the arms of the placid bay.

27

Trembled alone his bark canoe
As shocks of bursting lilies flew....

And he had spoke his soul of love
With a voice of eagle and of dove.

54

Of loud, strong pines his tongue was made;
His lips, soft blossoms in the shade,

That kissed her silver lips—her's cool
As lilies on his inmost pool

92

His cedar paddle, scented, red
He drew up from the lily bed;

All lily-locked, all lily-locked,
His light bark in the blossoms rocked.

117

Their cool lips round the sharp prow sang,
Their soft palms to the pale sides sprang,

With cedar paddle, scented, red,
He pushed out from the lily bed.

145

I.V.C
"The Lily Bed"

River tenses

Time changes on the river
becomes full of should haves
and would have beens

would be

A river if it were a part of speech would be a run-on sentence never stopping
when you think it should but going on forever until you're out of breath and
exasperated with its length you punctuate it silently as you follow it to the end.

had gone

If she had gone down the Saugeen in the spring, Isabella might have seen a raft
of cedar logs, fourteen feet wide and thirty feet long, break up on the rapids. Or
heard of the three men and two women who clung to the wreckage with bundles
of bedding and next to them, on the river's edge, a coop full of drowned
chickens stranded in a tree top.

would have

If Isabella were there, she would have seen a young man, the only one who could
swim, take off his clothes, hang them on the raft's wood, and tie some of the bed
cords around his waist. He is trying to swim to shore, but the current is too
strong. He tries again with the rope in his mouth. As he struggles, blood from
his lip stains the bed cords. He thrashes through the rapids and is swept into the
rocks. When he curses, the rope drops from his mouth. Although he makes it to
shore, the others can not follow. Naked, he walks along the river looking for
help. Dark comes. He stops to rest against a tree. He stands listening to the
snow fall around him, waiting for dawn.

might have

In the morning, he might have come upon Isabella's small group as they ate
oatmeal porridge. Isabella might have given him her blanket and what was left
in her bowl. And watched the snow melt on his shoulders as he ate. She might
even have followed him to the river.

Advice their fathers gave

Two women come together on the longest
and first day of summer.

They pick their way through riffles
glide past blue flags and vipers bugloss
envy the shoulder muscles
of grazing cows.

Because it is the Fathers Day weekend,
they try to remember their father's advice.
>   *Always pay cash.*
>   *Don't marry him. It will never work.*
>   *It's only a dream, don't be scared.*

Mostly their fathers weren't around.
They left when their daughters were still
asleep and returned after they had gone
to bed. The daughters wanted understanding,
but got advice about how to move
through the world of men.

Don't be scared, their fathers said,
>   *it's only a dream.*

They stay up late until summer comes.

Asleep by the river, they dream
in colour, brushing rain
from their eyes, falling down stairs,
but only Margaret remembers her dream.
>   A man old enough to be her father
>   arrives in a pickup truck
>   to carry her away.
She wakes up yelling
>   *I can't stop*
>   *we're going to crash!*
Yes you can, a voice says
>   backpaddle hard yes you can.

Sorting sounds

Asleep by the river   fast water   arrives

relentless noise   rivals

on opposite shores

constant   apologies

derived   from

the   wrong   reasons

must make sense

derive voices

from the river's babble

change the meaning

of small details

sorry to be

such a bother

a bother

bewilder

with noise

confuse

propose

small details

abandon

apologies

Dreams beside the Saugeen

Margaret dreams of two women.
The younger one, in white cotton pantaloons
with holes from crotch to knee, sits by the door,
a notebook resting on her lap.
The other one sits by the fire embroidering
a sampler, rocking back and forth.

The younger one chants to herself over and over

> *cedar paddle*
> *scented red*

The river speeds up with the night rains.

Susan dreams of white water—titanium white, bone
white, Titians buff white. Somewhere piano keys
are stroked. A woman with a needle in her hand
says to a girl in a white petticoat

> *When you play, I can hear the angels sing.*

Fishing 1

O love! art thou a silver fish.
Shy of the line and shy of gaffing.

I.V.C.
"Said the Canoe"

Isabella holds the fish gently in her hand, palm open,
fingers in the gills, the way her father had taught her.
On its side are six red dots just under the lateral line
running from eye to tail. Outlined in vivid blue, the red dots
notations of the river's voice.

This nerve path, fragile as a spine, runs fluid as warm ink.

Fins on the belly a bright orange, the one on top
spotted dark green. The eyes a dense black.
She rolls the fish over and looks at its back
to see how it would blend into the muted colours
of the river bed, the rocks, the refracted light.

Designed not to be noticed from above.
Isabella wishes they would let her fit
into the world this way.

She hears the neighbour's children taunting—
Va lan cy   Va lan cy
What kind of a name is that?

Her mother does not need to call her name.
She just thinks her and Isabella knows.

Isabella watches the fish gasp for air.
Its shudder in the palm of her hand echoed
by the trembling of her legs, unsteady
in the white current. Tired of being wary.
A life sticking to her hand.
She lowers the fish to the river. Holds it
under the surface, feels the trout's fear
as it waits for a breath.

Isabella holds hers until it takes off downstream.

Fishing 2

half in liquid   half in air

(Margaret is never
completely in one
place at the same time)

aired and watered
rivered and skyed
mirrored she blurs
and disappears
without a sound

she stalks, waits, watches
wonders why more women
don't walk in rivers
thinks its the silence
of their own thoughts
they can't stand

she takes small
water heavy steps
stumbles on slick rocks
red dragonflies dot the ferns
her arm raises above her head
then drops down
and the line feeds out
its arc unwinding
under the low branches
of a shoreline cedar
            upstream
                    a fish hovers
a small creature
you would think
she would be ashamed
to have quivering
on the end of her line
excited by the intense struggle
both of them hooked on each other
trembling

Mice

Swarms of white bellied deer mice rush across the table,
up the chair legs and snatch bits of meat pie.
Relentless as a flood. They can even gnaw through
the wooden bread box. Cats can't kill enough of them.
Isabella takes a bite of bread and her brother
catches one by the tail as it runs by her plate.
He dangles it in her face, throws it across the room.

At night they wake her pulling out strands of hair.
They nibble at her breasts and walk the length of her.
Her first lovers she calls them. Norse gods,
thin lips kissing her all over, whiskers tickling like beards.

She has seen the Ojibway sleep with mice and red fox
and has heard of the hawks they keep in their tents.
It is the nearness of these animals, she thinks,
and the sound of rivers, that we will miss the most.

Years later she will write
>   *Toronto, joy and peace!*
>   *....On lusty shoulders, still remember thee*
>   *Of my first cradle on the lilies' lap*
>   *In the dim woods....*

Deer

Driving out of the city, stuck in a long line of families
heading to their cottages, Margaret and Susan had listened
to the radio's insistent messages. When they stopped for gas,
Susan told Margaret about the interview with a fifteen
year old boy from Sudbury. He was explaining how a deer
had come crashing through the screen door into his bedroom.
The deer ran all over his room and him as he lay in bed.
He started screaming "There's a deer in my room!"
and his mother phoned the police. The lady at 911 just laughed
and said they'd send someone.

"Did you know," said Margaret, "that wintergreen lifesavers
give off sparks if you crush them between your teeth in the dark?"

"Sure," said Susan. "Didn't you used to do that?"

Margaret was feeling a bit like the deer.
Thrashing out of closed places.
Hoping the river would calm her.
Relieve obsessions.
Allow for small changes.

Twice down the Saugeen

All I know is
your name keeps me going
like a charm I keep saying it
over and over

Isabella Valancy Crawford
Isabella Valancy Crawford

When we stop to rest your name keeps me going

Susan Musgrave
Tarts and Muggers

Bundled up in beaver furs and fox skins
on top of a pile of hemlock boughs,
Isabella lies in the bottom of the canoe,
a blanket rolled up for her pillow. Her father
next to the Ojibway guide, who steers from the stern
with a long cedar paddle. The rest of the men
sit on low wooden seats suspended
from the ribs of the twenty five foot birch canoe,
red ochre symbols covering its white bark.

Fifty strokes a minute, so fast the water spray freezes
on her face. The suckers from the lake come up to spawn,
a silvery squirming clump.

After paddling a while, the men stop to light their pipes,
have a five-minute smoke, start paddling again.
After three pipes, they would have gone twelve miles.

The strong smell of tobacco hangs above her head,
and over that a hawk circles. The river pulls the canoe
towards the mouth, past thick stands of beech and maple
and red plum trees about to bloom.
        Flocks of wild pigeons darken the sun.

They stop on an island for tea and scones. To keep away
the mosquitoes, the guide lights a fire in the hollows.
His name might have meant the *sound of waves breaking on the rocks*
or maybe bursts of *thunder at a distance.*
        Isabella would have known.

How like to quivering flesh a stone may feel.

I.V.C.
"Malcolm's Katie"

unexplained bumps of water boiling up

wet pillows of stone

flat ledges where the river drops like stairs

the blue heron that keeps reappearing around the bend

brief acquaintances with cows

rare, so they think, yellow irises

three triangular islands compressing and speeding the flow

little time to choose

the rock they don't see until it's too late

the canoe drawing itself down a blue line

cliff swallows low on the water

a new understanding of the colour of mud

Abandoned

There's another bump, Susan calls from the stern.
What do you mean "a bump?"
I don't know, just a bump! A boil in the water.
You mean where the water rushes over the rocks?
No.
Can't you describe it?
No.

Head for the V! Margaret yells from the bow.
I am! I am! Susan shouts back.

Suddenly, the canoe turns sideways to the current, does a slow roll.

Margaret screams. Susan swears.

The canoe fills with water. They are both thrown out.
Susan manages to grab onto the stern
and is swept over to the rocks by the shore.

Come back here! Susan yells as Margaret is pulled under.

Part 4

And it was at that age . . . poetry arrived
in search of me. I don't know, I don't know where
it came from, from
winter or a river.

Pablo Neruda
"Poetry"
Where the Rain is Born

The river's voice

sorry   oh

so

sorry

didn't see the rock

can't come back   can't get out

can't breathe

skin separating from flesh

interrupted by stones

brown water a knife to my heart

I feel the blade harden

arc slowly

I hear it draw a line

widening

as the blade shortens

and comes back on itself

to ease out of me

out of this life

hanging over me

I taste my own smell   I hear a voice
no pain   the voice is saying   *no pain*

the sun shines through the blinds
covering your body
with soft grey stripes

it is twilight
a dark tunnel opens and closes
you watch your artery pulse
like the sound of waves
breaking, you say,
these sounds inside you

in between a rock and a hard place
a man's voice says
bleed to death
or end up paralyzed
without language
like the stones
you loved to gather
still   alive
at our mercy
bleeding hard

your breathing slows
your grab the electrodes
I help you rip them off
nurses rush in
sign this form
the machines wheel away
I wipe your mouth with a damp cloth

It's all right
your last words
or are they mine?

you release my hand
grab my sweater, pull me closer
your one good arm like a vise

breathing shallower

a short breath

a pause

another breath

a longer pause

your tongue grows fat in your mouth

no more breath

a vertical band of stained white

light rises from

behind your head

nothing but the taste of tears

eight of your heads

one for each decade

telescope to fill the vertical space

where the white light used to be

nothing but the rush of tears

you become all light

then half light, half woman

the lighter you become

the heavier I feel

tears so heavy they leave me weightless

a daughter, a mother

all in the same breath

all in this unbearably

powerful river

a ribbon of light

grows out of your head

and your head undulates

separates from your neck

and rides the arc of light

you leave me

a suggestion of shoulder

curved light

alone the next one

Propose

Margaret
I couldn't get my breath or tell which way was up.
The waves were rolling me over and over and I kept
scraping against the rocks. I couldn't stop.

Susan
Didn't you hear me yelling? *Come back here,*
I kept saying, *we've got to get the water out of this canoe!*
I knew I couldn't hold on to it much longer myself.
You left me alone.

| *Margaret* | *Susan* |
| I thought I heard a voice. | I felt abandoned. |

Margaret
First it sounded like stones rolling across the bottom,
then willow branches rustling. Then it became clearer.
It's all right the voice kept saying. *It's all right.*
The next thing I knew, you were saying my name
and I was wiping the mud from my eyes.

Susan:	*Margaret*
I'm glad you're all right.	Do you think I am?
I thought I'd lost you.	No, I did that myself.

Susan
Don't you think it's about time you learned how to read the water,
instead of just books?

Margaret
Maybe, that is, if you'll teach me.
But first, you've got to promise me something.
Remember how two or three times a week
our mothers used to get together for drinks?

Saga blue

If it was at my mother's house
she would have the martinis chilled
by five o'clock, just when your mother
would be opening the door of her aqua blue
Chevy, reaching across the seat for her cane
painted with parrots and snakes,
in the days when they both had husbands
and their children still lived at home.

Around five most summer evenings
I find myself in the back yard garden
walking past the gravestone idol
your father brought back from Peru.
The same stone idol my mother planted
among her lilies, where she could gaze
at this marker of death as she picked their blooms
eyes squinting in a moon-shaped face
   hers puffed up with cortisone
   his carved by unknown hands
both she and the stone taking root
in foreign lands. And I can't help
but wonder how you and I will do
when the time comes.

By now our mothers would be commenting
on the rapid growth of white pines
and their hopes for grandchildren,
pouring each other another martini.
From the lily bed, the idol stares back
and forth across centuries
of massacre and destruction.
Our mothers knew this idol
like all objects of desire
had been stolen, yet they needed
the beauty of ruined cultures
as much as they did old friends.

My mother would have spread saga blue,
your mother's favourite cheese,
offering from the palm of her hand
a round cracker balanced as gently
as the secret that lay between them,
the pact they had made
to be there for each other
for you never know how it will come,
where your family will be,
if you will have the strength.

But you do know what doctors
are sworn to do and you know your life
means more than that.

After all, what could they do if one of us
opens a bottle taped under the bed
within easy reach of arthritic fingers
and misreads the label that says
take two before bedtime.

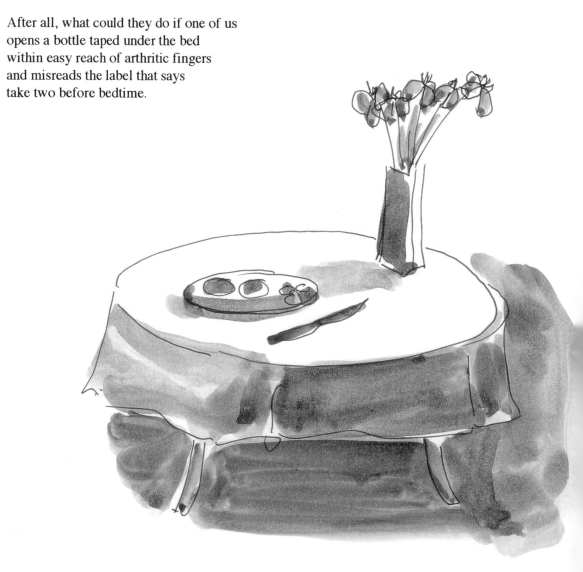

It is there, growing

At first I thought reading the river meant I should be its master.
I would match its speed with my cunning
       avoid ledges and souse holes
       slip around boulders, profit from eddies.

That is, until I dreamed   smelled
            swallowed the river

    this river that rushed
first beneath then over then through me.

I have memorized the chant Susan taught me

        angle   motion   tilt

it's the way you approach the current—
unless you add momentum and lean downstream
almost simultaneously and in that order—*angle-motion-tilt*
       you're done for

     (Go at it slant, as Emily Dickinson said)

Susan says
      wait until the bow crosses the eddy line and draw hard

      use cross draws so you don't lose time changing hands

      and back ferries, point the stern where you want to go
      and let the current slip you sideways across the river

         how all these years I've been living
         next to a great lake's constant mass,
          invisible from within the city
          as I have let myself become.

      And somehow I knew I needed a river

with its beginning, middle and end
to remind me of an essence I had lost
             was it at thirteen
             or twenty-four or just
a few years ago that I began to feel
stretched so tight
             and worn away
                          from myself.

             I have always headed backwards
into another woman's life
                   to look for myself
             but never have I looked through a river.

And never before have I enjoyed the precision during that second or two
             when you can choose
             which side of the rock to aim for
because you are going slower than the current and because
             you know   the way to avoid the rock
                   is to head directly for it
                                because it is the current that is in charge
and really, all we can do
                   is be aware of its force
back up when we're going too fast
             and when we get off balance
                          remember not to grab the gunwales
                                but reach out for the river
slap its softness
                   brace long and low into the turn
             because the success of this maneuver
                          depends on trusting
                                your weight
                                        to the river.

             I stand here feeling the river's power
                          sensing my own
                   knowing it is there, growing.

Connections

She will turn again and come to meet me.

I.V.C.

the sun casts their shadow thin across the river

they stand looking at a suspended line of shoulder

rare, so they think, yellow irises

a white trout blurring the line of shoulder

with little time to choose

they wonder if there will ever be someone

who sees them standing here at the edge of memory

reaching for those that are missing

a mother, a river, a self

leaning into the turn of life

just at the moment of recall

when the past and present are one

Said the river—two

I trickle, boil
babble, cascade.
I swirl into eddies,
meander, and overflow.
I propose and abandon.
I never apologize.
I convey, I bathe and I soothe.
I am the one who gives
and the one who takes away.

I can speak in rhyme
(if you know how to listen)
of beginnings and ends
and all that middle
of heads and moss
of ferns and mouths.
Of long journeys that take only one of your days
or a whole stream of lives.
Of the way you turn backwards to find out
where you're going, or the way you yearn
for my speed and passion, ignoring the signs I post
because they're not in your language but
in River, a tongue you're just learning to speak.

I can make you forget what you have learned.
I am taboo and I am sacred.
I am the first blood of your mother.
I consume all sins and remake
your flesh into a little child's.
I am where you sit down beside
what memories you have left
and weep. I am lonely
from being too often touched.

But I will be all right only
if I have a constant source.
You are that source.
You are the fire that burns.
You are the tiger that consumes.
You are the river.

Main Characters

Isabella Valancy Crawford. Born in Dublin in 1850. Immigrated to Paisley, Ontario when she was eight years old and had only 28 more years to live—most of them close to poverty, in cheap rooming houses and unheated parlours, where she wrote fairy tales, stories and poems. James Reaney, in his introduction to the reprinted edition of Isabella's collected poems, says "her life resembles a trial-run for the imagination in this country, and because the run was made and dared it has been much easier since."

Sydney Scott Crawford. Mother of Isabella and 12 other children (or some say 11). Most died of the fever, or the family's inherited heart disease. After her husband's death, she was supported mainly by Isabella's writing. No photographs of Isabella's parents have been found. The portrait opposite is of an "unknown woman" painted by an unknown artist, sometime in the nineteenth century.

Dr. Stephen Dennis Crawford. Isabella's father. Accused of embezzling money from the Town of Paisley, for which he was appointed treasurer. Reputed to have falsified his medical credentials and to have drunk too much milk punch, although he was thought to be very clever when sober. Represented by the photo of an unidentified gentleman found in the Baldwin Room's archives.

Margaret Anshen. Born in North Carolina in 1946. Immigrated to Toronto, Ontario when she was ten years old. Became a librarian because she felt safe only with books. Driving through the countryside, she chances upon a historical plaque honouring Isabella Valancy Crawford and becomes obsessed with the poet's life and work. She finds herself discovering, the similarities of their lives.

Sophie Anshen. Margaret's mother, who died at the age of 81, a few years after *Dr. Milton Anshen,* Margaret's father, passed away and a few years before Margaret began her search for Isabella. Both Sophie and Margaret are what used to be called "late bloomers." In their late forties, from deep inside, a knot unravels.

Susan LaFlame. Born in Manitoba in 1946 and currently living in her Toronto studio on King St. West. Susan is a visual artist mainly known for her landscapes painted from memory. She and Margaret became friends when they were in grade school. Susan used to talk Margaret into skipping class to canoe over to the Toronto islands for the day.

Samuel Orchard. Built a raft of cedar logs in Walkerton and floated down the Saugeen River with his family, looking for a hardwood forest of beech, maple and elm that would mean good soil. He landed where the Saugeen and Teeswater Rivers came together and founded the town of Paisley .

Saugeen River. Lined with weeping willows and cows, runs mostly through farmland until it empties into Lake Huron. Swallows nest in its sandy banks and speckled, brown and rainbow trout still live in its waters. Isabella probably accompanied her father down this river on his visits to the Saugeen Indians. The kind of river you could find yourself in.

Don River. In the heart of Toronto, a source of anxiety for city planners, who have to plan for floods that might occur in the wake of hurricanes. No longer a source of much else, except an annual spring canoe race and various movements to bring back the Don. How time changes rivers. Our past and future may be indicated by them.

Afterwords

I first met Isabella Valancy Crawford beside the Saugeen River, in front of her historical plaque in Paisley, Ontario. I was looking for good places to fly fish. She had been dead for a hundred years.

I'd never seen a historical plaque dedicated to a woman poet, only to war heros and explorers. I knew I had to find out more about her. As I researched her in libraries, archives and anthologies, I began to discover many parallels between her life and mine. We loved the sensuality of language and canoes. Knew the importance of wilderness. Studied Latin and French. Self-published our poems in large print runs. We were both immigrants to Canada. She started out in rural Ontario and ended up in Toronto. I did the reverse. Our fathers were doctors. Our mothers were wives.

Very little is known of the details of Isabella's life. In those days, well-educated women such as Catherine Parr Traill and Susanna Moodie kept journals. But all that was found in the rooming house where Isabella died, was a trunk full of manuscripts, most rejected by publishers.

In fact, long after *Said the River* was written, I found out that John W. Garvin, who first published Isabella's collected poems in 1905, paid a visit to Isabella's third floor flat sometime after she had died. He was horrified to discover that her poems and papers were being used as kindling. The manuscripts Garvin rescued eventually found their way to the Lorne Pierce Collection at Queens University in Kingston, Ontario.

So what I suspected had actually happened. Many of Isabella's papers had been burnt. Isabella herself could have left such instructions. Or there could have been a shortage of kindling coupled with a lack of regard for a poet's work. I came up with another possibility.

I suspected that Isabella, a Victorian spinster, had begun to develop a unique voice and had started to write truths that would be horrifying, or at the very least—embarrassing, to her family. That's when I got the idea to create a series of "burnt poems" that she might have written. They would have been tied with ribbons and kept under her bed.

I began to take the scarce facts of her life and invent my own truth from them. But how to put it all together? Visual artist, long-time friend and canoeist Janis Hoogstraten and I had talked of doing a book together. Taking a trip down the Saugeen River seemed like the ideal way to create this book, as it required a leisurely paddle—with time to write and draw.

We started meeting for lunch, (another favourite pastime) to plan our canoe trip down the Saugeen. I'm not sure what I expected to find. I know Janis was more interested in fishing and drawing, than in some Victorian poet. I wanted to see if I could feel Isabella's spirit—by canoeing down the same river she must have travelled. Planned as a three day trip, we sped down the river in just one day, with no time to write or draw. Because of heavy rains, the river was as fast and as high as it was during spring runoff.

Back in the city, we traded drafts of poems and drawings. A revised line of a poem would evoke a new drawing. This new drawing would call for a whole new poem. Exchanges of poems and drawings went on for months, until we reached master lithographer Don Holman's deadline and had to go to print. The first edition of this book was hand-printed in a limited edition by the University of Toronto's Scarborough Campus Fine Arts Department under the direction of Holman, with the assistance of Michael Campbell.

Although *Said the River* is based on the historical record of rivers, places and persons living and dead, this is a work of fiction.

TIMELINE

1845   The potato blight hits Ireland again and "the Great Famine" sent many people to the new world.

1850   Isabella born in Dublin, Ireland.

The HMS Enterprise & HMS Investigator leave England on the latest search for the explorer Sir John Franklin.

1851   Simon Orchard floats down the Saugeen River, lands where two rivers join and builds a shack from the boards of his raft, starting the town of Paisley.

1852   Susanna Moodie publishes *Roughing it in the Bush*.

1856   After unsuccessful attempts to settle in the U.S. and Australia, Dr. Crawford finally emigrates to Paisley, Ontario, and brings his family to Canada the following year.

1859   Charles Darwin publishes *Origin of Species*.

1860   Abraham Lincoln is elected President. South Carolina secedes. 60% of Canadian immigrants are Irish.

1861   Elizabeth Barrett Browning dies. The Crawfords leave Paisley, apparently under a cloud. Dr. Crawford served as Elderslie Township's treasurer, and in 1863 was sued for $500 missing from the township accounts.

1862   Henry David Thoreau dies. Photosynthesis is discovered. The Crawford family is discovered "poorly off" in a village north of Kingston by Robert Strickland and his brother (nephews of Susanna Moodie and Catherine Parr Traill). The Stricklands persuade Dr. Crawford to move to Lakefield, just north of Peterborough.

1865   *Alice's Adventures in Wonderland* is published.
Lincoln assassinated.

1867   British North America act establishes the Dominion of Canada.

1869	The Crawford family moves from Lakefield to Peterborough. Dr. Crawford's practice and the family fortunes decline steadily over the next six years.
	First Red River Rebellion under Louis Riel.
	Eaton's new store opens on Yonge St., Toronto.
1870	A Toronto man is jailed 10 days for stealing a turkey and spends each alternate day in solitary confinement.
1870-75	Isabella begins to publish poems and stories both in Canada and the U.S. She wins a $600 prize for a short story "Winona, the Indian Queen," and the prize-giving corporation goes bankrupt after paying only one installment.
1875	Dr. Crawford dies on July 3.
1876	Alexander Graham Bell receives the world's first long distance telephone call from Brantford to Paris, Ontario.
	Emma Naomi, Isabella's last surviving sister, dies January 20. Stephen, her 16-year old brother, leaves Peterborough to work in the Algoma region. In the summer, Isabella and her mother move to Toronto and spend the next ten and a half years living in a series of boarding houses, barely supported by Isabella's writing.
	Little Big Horn, Custer's last stand.
1876-79	No record has been found of any Canadian publication during these three years. Crawford probably spends this time writing for American magazines.
1878	September 14, a major flood causes Toronto's Don River to rise more than eight feet.
1879	Crawford begins to publish in Canada again. Many of her works appear in are published in the *Globe* and *Telegram* newspapers in Toronto.
1880	The first woman doctor, Dr. Emily Howard Stoe, is admitted to practise in Ontario.

1884	Crawford self-publishes her only book, *Old Spookses' Pass, Malcom's Katie and Other Poems*. One thousand copies are printed, but only 50 are sold.
	First votes for women in Ontario municipal elections.
1887	Isabella Crawford dies suddenly of a heart attack, or some say, a broken heart, on February 12. She is buried in Peterborough.
	"Saturday Night" magazine is founded. Canadian Pacific Railway formally opens.
1894.	Death of Crawford's mother, on March 20 at the age of eighty. Buried next to her daughter in Little Lake Cemetery, Peterborough.

Acknowledgements

I'd like to thank Don Holman for his support. This book has always been dedicated to him.

Nor would it have been possible without Janis Hoogstraten's canoeing skills and wild sense of humour, which got us through numerous rapids and revisions.

Thanks to readers Stuart McKinnon, Susan Gibson, and Merike Lugus, whose comments I value. And to the Ontario Arts Council for financial assistance from their Writers' Reserve Program.

I'm grateful to the staff at the Metropolitan Toronto Reference Library and the Durham Public Library and to all the people who have written about Isabella. Elizabeth McNeill Galvin's *Isabella Valancy Crawford, We scarcely Knew Her* is a good place to start.

I am also grateful to Penumbra Press for giving Janis and me the chance to continue exploring the experiences we shared, along with those we imagined. This edition of *Said the River* contains many new poems (as well as revisions of the original ones) and a whole new set of drawings designed to be reproduced in black and white. One doesn't often get a second chance to get it right.

Credits

Photograph of Isabella from *The Collected Poems of Isabella Valancy Crawford*, Edited by J.W. Garvin, G.A., Toronto, William Briggs, 1905

Photographs representing Sydney Scott Crawford and Dr. Stephen Dennis Crawford from the Baldwin Room archives, Metropolitan Toronto Reference Library.

Photographs of Margaret and Sophie Anshen and Susan LaFlame from family albums.

Photograph of Samuel Orchard from *A History of Bruce County*

Photograph of the Saugeen River by Judy Lowry

Photograph of the Don River from *The Task Force to Take Back the Don*

SAID THE RIVER

photo credit: Ira Zingraff

Poems by Liz Zetlin

Drawings by Janis Hoogstraten